Detroit

Detroit

A Downtown America Book

Chanda K. Zimmerman

Dillon Press, Inc.   Minneapolis, MN 55415

Library of Congress Cataloging-in-Publication Data

Zimmerman, Chanda K.
    Detroit / by Chanda K. Zimmerman.
        p.   cm. — (A Downtown America book)
    Includes index.
    Summary: Explores Detroit as an industrial center and a major port; describes the city's heritage, its people, and their ethnic backgrounds; and highlights places and sites of special interest to children.
    ISBN 0-87518-409-X
    1. Detroit (Mich.)—Juvenile literature.   [1. Detroit (Mich.)]
I. Title.   II. Series.
F474.D44Z56   1989
977.4'34—dc 19   88-35914
                                                             CIP
                                                             AC

© 1989 by Dillon Press, Inc. All rights reserved

Dillon Press, Inc., 242 Portland Avenue South
Minneapolis, Minnesota 55415

Printed in the United States of America
1 2 3 4 5 6 7 8 9 10 98 97 96 95 94 93 92 91 90 89

Photographic Acknowledgments

The photographs are reproduced through the courtesy of Dennis Cox; Dale Fisher; the Metropolitan Detroit Convention and Visitor's Bureau; the Michigan Department of Natural Resources (David Kenyon); the Michigan State Travel Bureau; and Robert Stewart. Cover photograph by Dale Fisher.

Contents

Fast Facts about Detroit

Detroit: The Motor City; Motown; Arsenal of Democracy; City of Champions

Location: Michigan's lower peninsula along the Detroit River between Lake St. Clair and Lake Erie; Windsor, Canada lies across the river

Area: City, 140 square miles (363 square kilometers); consolidated metropolitan area, 5,312 square miles (13,758 square kilometers)

Population (1986 estimate*): City, 1,086,220; consolidated metropolitan area, 4,609,700

Major Population Groups: Blacks, Canadians, English, Germans, Irish, Italians, Poles, Greeks

Altitude: 581 feet (177 meters) above sea level at Detroit River

Climate: Average mean temperature is 26.2°F (-4°C) in January, 73.3°F (23°C) in July; humid in summer, cold and snowy in winter

Founding Date: July 24, 1701; incorporated as a city in 1815

City Flag: In quarters: a blue field with white stars of the American flag in upper left corner; red and white stripes in lower right corner; three gold British lions on a red background in upper right corner; gold French fleur-de-lis on a white background in lower left corner; the city seal in center

City Seal: A circular design with two figures in togas at center; behind them on right, early buildings, on left, flames to represent the great fire; two mottos above and below: *Speramus Meliora* and *Resurget Cineribus* ("We hope for better things" and "It will rise from its ashes")

Form of Government: Mayor and nine city council members with strong executive power reserved for the mayor

Important Industries: Automobiles, metal and metal products, chemicals, shipping, advertising, breweries, retailers

*U.S. Bureau of the Census 1988 population estimates available in fall 1989; official 1990 census figures available in 1991-92.

Festivals and Parades

March: Maple Syrup Festival at Cranbrook Educational Facility, Bloomfield Hills

April: Civil War Days at Historic Fort Wayne; International Strawberry Festival in Hamtramck

May: The Riverfront Ethnic Festivals begin; summer events at Chene Park; International Festival at University Cultural Center in Detroit

June: Spirit of Detroit-Budweiser Thunderboat Championship on Detroit River; Detroit Grand Prix Formula I race; Muzzleloaders Festival at Greenfield Village; beginning of Freedom Festival between Detroit and Windsor, Canada

July: Freedom Festival continues; French Festival in Detroit

August: State Fair at Fairgrounds in Detroit

September: Stroh's Montreux Jazz Festival; Hamtramck Polish Festival; Autumn Harvest Festival at Greenfield Village; Labor Day parades in many communities

October: Cider time festivals at many cider mills

November: Michigan Thanksgiving Day Parade; Festival of Trees in Detroit

December: Festival of Christmas at Greenfield Village

For further information about festivals and parades, see agencies listed on page 56.

United States

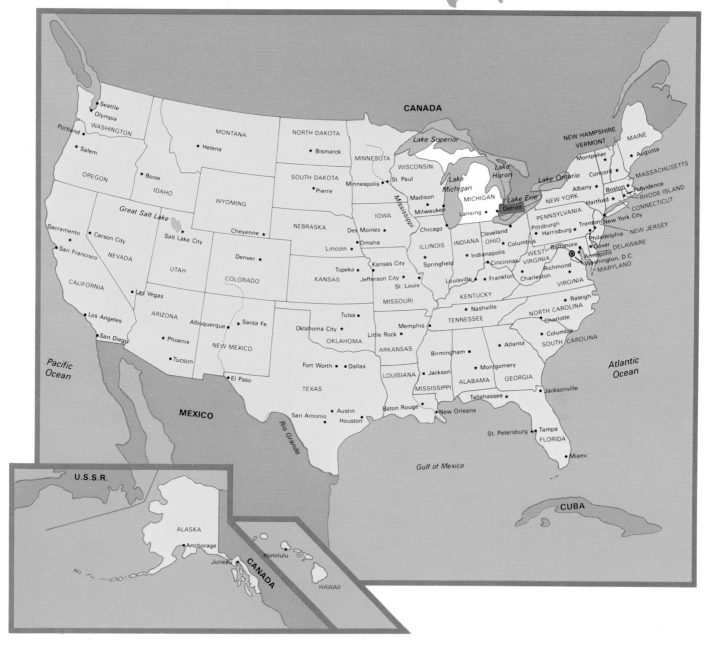

Detroit

MICHIGAN

Detroit ●

N

MICHIGAN

WAYNE COUNTY

EIGHT MILE ROAD

OUTER DRIVE

McNICHOLS ROAD

LIVERNOIS AVENUE

CHRYSLER FREEWAY

CONANT AVENUE

VAN DYKE AVENUE

HOOVER AVENUE

GRATIOT AVENUE

LAKE SHORE DRIVE

④

GRAND RIVER AVENUE

JOHN C. LODGE FREEWAY

WOODWARD AVENUE

HAMTRAMCK

OUTER DRIVE

I-94

I-96

PLYMOUTH ROAD

LAKE SAINT CLAIR

SOUTHFIELD FREEWAY

SHAEFER HIGHWAY

JEFFRIES FREEWAY

MACK AVENUE

RIVER ROUGE PARK

②

⑨

DETROIT

UNITED STATES
CANADA

TELEGRAPH ROAD

EDSEL FORD FREEWAY

⑦

③

JEFFERSON EAST

BELLE ISLE PARK

⑥

DEARBORN

MICHIGAN AVENUE

⑧

①

GREEKTOWN

Windsor

OUTER DRIVE

⑤

I-94

FISHER FREEWAY

JEFFERSON WEST

I-75

JEFFERSON WEST

DETROIT RIVER

miles

0   1¼   2½   5

0   5

kilometers

Points of Interest

① Hart Plaza
② University Cultural Center (Museum of African-American History, Detroit Science Center, Institute of Arts)
③ Renaissance Center
④ University of Detroit
⑤ Henry Ford Museum/Greenfield Village
⑥ Dossin Great Lakes Museum
⑦ Tiger Stadium
⑧ Cobo Hall
⑨ Wayne State University

An aerial view of downtown Detroit.

1

The Motor City—and More

What do you think of when someone says "Detroit?" Most people think of cars. Detroit, sometimes called the Motor City, is the center for major automobile companies such as General Motors, Ford Motor Company, and Chrysler Corporation. Together, they are known as the Big Three of the auto industry, and it is hard to go anywhere in Detroit without feeling their presence. Yet there is much more to Detroit than just large car companies.

Detroit is the largest city in Michigan and the sixth largest in the United States. More than one million people live in the city, and 4.6 million in the much larger metropolitan area, which covers parts of seven counties.

Detroit's place on the map has played an important part in the city's history. The State of Michigan has two sections, the Upper Peninsula and the

This map shows Detroit's location at the base of the "thumb" in Michigan's Lower Peninsula.

Lower Peninsula. The lower part of Michigan looks like a giant mitten, and Detroit lies at the base of the thumb. In fact, if you ask Detroiters how to get somewhere else in the state, they may hold up their hand and use it just like a map.

Detroit rises along the edge of the Detroit River. Many of the city's best-known places—parks, island playgrounds, beautiful neighborhoods, and historic sites—are closest to the river. New, stunning skyscrapers and the rebuilding of some famous down-

St. Josaphat Church's spire rises among modern buildings such as Detroit's Renaissance Center.

town areas have given Detroit a fresh, sparkling face. Ultramodern hotels and office buildings share the skyline with old-fashioned brick skyscrapers decorated with the designs of the 1920s and 1930s. Down below and tucked between their tall neighbors are smaller storefronts and historic stone churches with elegant spires.

Yet, high above this urban setting, peregrine falcons soar among the skyscrapers. The falcons were placed here by wildlife experts, who hope they will nest and raise families in the city.

A conservation officer holds a young peregrine falcon before releasing it in the city.

From the river's edge, the metropolitan area spreads to the west, north, and south over three counties. In fact, many of the people who use the city's famous freeways are on their way to or from the suburbs that circle Detroit. Some may drive as long as an hour or more to get home.

The spiderweb of freeways runs into the city from several directions. On work days, this high-speed network of roads is packed with cars as people try to get to and from the many businesses in downtown Detroit. Detroit is known for its traffic jams, and people like to drive bumper-to-bumper. In the winter, it's not unusual to hear of dozens of cars involved in one accident because of bad weather. Although Detroit's winters can be very

In this view, the northern end of the Detroit River connects with the waters of Lake Saint Clair. A bridge connects the city to Belle Isle.

cold with lots of snow, the city clears the roads quickly, and the cars keep moving.

Another route that gets a lot of traffic is the Detroit River, a vital waterway that connects Lake Saint Clair and Lake Erie. Above Lake Saint Clair is the Saint Clair River, which leads to Lake Huron. The Detroit River is wide enough and deep enough to allow large ships to pass between the lakes. It helps link all the Great Lakes to the Atlantic Ocean through the Saint Lawrence Seaway.

A large freighter is loaded with cargo at the Detroit Harbor Terminal.

Across the Detroit River is the Canadian city of Windsor. The two cities are connected by a tunnel beneath the river and the Ambassador Bridge over the water. The bridge is beautiful at night when thousands of sparkling lights dangle from its cables.

Detroit and Windsor have a close and special relationship. Many people live in one city and work in the other. Since it is easy to cross the border, Detroiters can shop and eat lunch in Windsor in an "English" atmosphere, and then be back in Detroit for dinner at Greektown!

Detroit has much in common with its Canadian neighbors. Both cities claim a French and English heritage. Today, they work together with their respective nations to protect the

Flags fly in a Windsor park across the Detroit River from the Renaissance Center.

Detroit River, the Great Lakes, the environment, and the jobs of people on both sides of the border.

In late June and early July, the two cities jointly celebrate the birthdays of Canada and the United States. For about two weeks, they hold The International Freedom Festival. Near the Fourth of July, they shoot off more than eight tons of fireworks from a barge on the river, showering both cities in red, white, and blue.

Detroit is a city with many different faces. People who live in other parts of the United States often think of Detroit as a decaying city with a high crime rate. Like any large industrial city, Detroit does have its share of rundown buildings and crime-ridden neighborhoods. Yet it is also a city working hard to change its image and to overcome its problems.

Fireworks explode above the Detroit River during the International Freedom Festival.

Detroiters in traditional costumes march during the Michigan Thanksgiving Day Parade.

2

The International City

People have come to Detroit from all over the world. In most of the city's neighborhoods, there is a mixture of people from many different backgrounds. Detroit grew through the hard work of the immigrants who came looking for a better life. In many ways, they built the city, and without them Detroit would never have become as large an urban center as it is.

The French were the first to come to Detroit. In 1701, a group of French settlers led by Antoine de la Mothe Cadillac built a fort on the Detroit River. The famous Cadillac car is named after this Frenchman. About sixty years later, the British seized the fort, now an important fur-trading post, during the French and Indian War. In 1778, during the Revolutionary War, British forces began to build another fort at the same site.

Even after the American Revolution, the British kept control of the fort and the Michigan fur trade. They refused to surrender to American forces until 1796. Today, Detroit remembers its beginnings with the city's flag, which combines the symbols of all three nations—the French *fleur-de-lis*, the English lion, and the American Stars and Stripes. After the British, the French, and the Americans had settled the question of who owned Detroit, many people from other countries began to arrive.

By the year 1900, one of every three Detroiters was a foreign-born immigrant, and most of the city's schoolchildren had foreign-born parents. Many of the immigrants were unskilled workers without much education. Today, the immigration continues, but many of the newcomers are students, doctors, businesspeople, and artists.

Germans were one of the largest, earliest groups of immigrants to come to Detroit. Later, Russians, Hungarians, and Austrians arrived. Throughout the city's early history, Poles also came in large numbers.

In fact, Polish traditions in Detroit are so strong that sometimes it seems as if the whole city is Polish. Sooner or later, everyone in Detroit samples Polish food and tries to dance the polka, a traditional Polish dance. In Hamtramck, which was settled by Polish immigrants, the Strawberry Festival features wonderful Polish music and food. Detroiters come from all over the city to have fun at this popular celebration.

One of Detroit's many ethnic groups thrives in the neighborhood called Greektown. The city has had an active Greek community since the early 1900s. Today, this area is full of restaurants that serve some of the finest food in Detroit.

Greektown, located in the older part of the city, attracts many people for dining and entertainment. On evenings and weekends, it becomes so crowded that drivers no longer attempt to pass through the streets. The "traffic" changes to crowds who walk along the streets as well as the sidewalks. While this area has other kinds of restaurants, it is best known for the Greek restaurants and baker-

A Greektown merchant reads a Greek newspaper published in Detroit.

ies. At one restaurant, the traditional entertainment is provided by belly dancers.

In recent years, other ethnic groups from the Middle East, India, Mexico, and Latin America have come to Detroit in large numbers. The metropolitan area has one of the largest populations of Arabs outside of the Middle East. Smaller groups from Japan, China, the Netherlands, Czechoslovakia, Romania, and many other nations also call the city home. In addition, Detroit has a large Italian and Jewish population. There are so many different ethnic groups that it's hard to keep track of them all!

The best way to experience the heritage of these Detroiters is to attend the Riverfront Festivals, which are held all summer long at Hart Plaza. Each festival features a different ethnic group demonstrating its traditional food, dances, music, and costumes.

Detroit is also known for its large population of black Americans, many of whom came to the city from the South in the 1940s and 1950s. The number who live within the city itself is increasing rapidly. Today, two of every three Detroiters are black.

Before the Civil War, many black Americans traveled through Detroit on their way to freedom in Canada. The Underground Railroad was a secret route taken by escaped slaves, made up of safe way stations where they could stay on their journey north. Detroit was one of the last stops on the "railroad." From here, it was easy to

A young woman celebrates her Ukrainian heritage at one of Detroit's Riverfront Festivals.

get to Canada. At the Museum of African-American History at the Wayne State University Cultural Center, visitors can see how the Underground Railroad worked.

Although many blacks went to Canada, others made Detroit their home. Later, as their numbers grew, conflicts developed between the city's black citizens and white ethnic groups. In 1943, fighting between blacks and whites led to a riot in which 34 people were killed. But the riots of 1967 were the worst, and the scars they left are still fresh in the memory of Detroiters. The riots occurred because of racial conflicts, poverty, and discrimination against blacks in jobs and housing. During this week of looting and burning in black neighborhoods, 43 people

Detroiters at a city park by the river.

died, and 7,000 were arrested for taking part in the violence.

Although the racial conflicts in Detroit have not ended, progress has been made. Since the riots of 1967, the citizens of Detroit have often led the nation in the struggle for civil rights. They formed New Detroit Inc. and other civic groups to improve race relations, education, housing, and jobs. Many black Detroiters now hold powerful positions in the city and state government. Others have made important contributions in the business community and the arts.

In fact, Detroit's black singing stars such as Diana Ross created what is still called the MoTown Sound in the music world. Thanks to their talents and local producers, a recording industry developed in the city in the 1960s and 1970s.

In parts of Detroit, the old is giving way to the new. People whose parents once fled the city for the suburbs now are moving back downtown. In the riverfront area, old warehouses along the river have been turned into restaurants and nightclubs. Nearby, shops, apartments, and condominiums have been built. Bricktown—named for the brickwork on its buildings—is another neighborhood that has been rebuilt and restored. In New Center, important businesses have opened offices, and new residents now live nearby. Some people call this area a "city within a city." In many other parts of town, old buildings have been restored, and people are beginning to

appreciate the style of their old-fashioned architecture.

Detroit today is a city that has suffered from years of decay and neglect. Yet it is also a city that has begun to renew itself. Much still needs to change in Detroit, but Detroiters are determined to build a new and better future for their city.

Skaters skim across the ice at Hart Plaza by the Renaissance Center.

River Rouge has been an important industrial area in Detroit during the twentieth century.

3

Made in Detroit

For most of the twentieth century, Detroiters have depended on the automobile industry for jobs. Many people were involved in creating the great automobile companies, but one of the most successful was Henry Ford, founder of Ford Motor Company. Ford, John and Horace Dodge, and Ransom E. Olds helped make Detroit the center of the U.S. auto industry.

Once, during World War II, Detroit stopped making cars completely. Instead, the carmakers began to build tanks, trucks, and planes for the war effort, and Detroit became famous around the world as the Arsenal of Democracy. Without the city's contribution, America and its allies might have lost the war.

After the war, Detroit again manufactured cars day and night in huge factories. Many of the same factories

Workers on an automobile assembly line in Detroit.

are still producing automobiles today.

Almost all of the car workers joined the United Auto Workers (UAW) trade union, which was founded in Detroit in 1935. Today, the UAW is still one of the world's largest and most powerful labor or-ganizations. When the UAW talks, people listen, especially in Detroit.

Detroit's dependence on the au-tomobile industry became a serious problem in the late 1970s and 1980s. As the nation went through hard eco-nomic times and companies expanded to other parts of the world, the big automobile factories around Detroit began to close. Thousands of people suddenly lost their jobs. Even small businesses suffered, because workers without jobs could not afford to buy from them. Today, the city's economy is more stable, and Detroiters have begun to realize that other industries are just as important as the carmakers.

The Detroit River is the center for one of those industries. Detroit, a city of ships, is a gateway for shipping between the eastern and western Great Lakes ports. The river is one of the world's busiest inland waterways. Huge freighters from around the world share the river with thousands of small pleasure boats.

Every year, 100 million tons of cargo move up and down the Detroit River, bound for more than 200 ports around the world. The river is so busy that the U.S. Post Office has kept a ship to deliver mail to passing freighters since 1894. Today, the ship even has its own zipcode.

Along with the big ships, Detroit boasts one of the largest collections of recreational boats in the world. The U.S. Coast Guard, which patrols the river as part of the U.S./Canadian border, estimates that more than 250,000 pleasure boats travel the water between Lake Saint Clair and Lake Erie. Detroiters enjoy sailing, cruising the river in powerboats, and fishing in simple rowboats.

Mixed in with the small pleasure boats are the huge freighters and tug-

A freighter on the Detroit River passes by downtown Detroit.

During the winter, wind-driven iceboats replace the freighters on the river.

boats. They all share the Detroit River, along with the ships of the Coast Guard and state conservation officers. In the winter, iceboats replace the freighters because the Great Lakes are closed to shipping for the winter months.

Before the shipping season ends, strong storms on the Great Lakes sometimes threaten even the big ships. Many freighters and their crews have sunk during such late autumn storms.

The Old Mariner's Church in downtown Detroit was built in the

The Old Mariner's Church stands near the huge Renaissance Center.

A lifeboat from the *Edmund Fitzgerald,* which sank during a storm on Lake Superior.

early 1800s. Now, it stands in the shadow of Detroit's famous Renaissance Center, which includes a 73-story hotel, four office buildings, and a shopping center. Every year, people gather at the church to remember those who have lost their lives on the Great Lakes. Popular singer Gordon Lightfoot often comes to sing his song about the *Edmund Fitzgerald,* a ship that vanished on Lake Superior during a fall storm in 1975.

Another important industry in Detroit is metal parts manufacturing.

The campus of Wayne State University in Detroit.

Metal parts manufacturers produce springs, screws, drills, wire, and dies, which are used to shape parts and objects. The carmakers depend on many of these small metal parts companies for parts that are used in building a car.

Since the companies that manufacture products need advertising agencies to help sell them, Detroit became an advertising center. Some advertising agencies employ hundreds of people, while others are very small.

Large computer manufacturers have also built plants in Detroit. Today, there are computer-related companies around the city, and Detroit is working hard to attract and promote more of these high-technology businesses.

Along with industry, education

will play a big role in the city's future. Detroit has about 300 schools, including several fine private schools such as Cranbrook Educational Facility. The Cranbrook Estate is internationally known as a center for the arts and sciences. It has its own art and science museums, and a planetarium. Students can study with respected teachers from around the world in the peaceful setting of a Tudor mansion, Scandinavian-style academies, and acres of magnificent gardens.

Detroit is also home to several universities, such as Wayne State University and the University of Detroit. The University of Michigan, although located in nearby Ann Arbor, was founded in Detroit in 1817.

Today, the city still needs to develop different kinds of industry. Detroit is becoming much more than the Motor City, but it still has much work to do to develop new products "made in Detroit."

Classic cars and planes in the exhibit of American transportation at the Henry Ford Museum.

4

Detroit—Just for Fun

In Detroit, things to do for fun begin with cars. Many people around the world share Detroiters' interest in cars and come to see them in the Motor City. The Detroit Auto Show is the yearly showcase for the automobile manufacturers and displays models of the past, present, and future. For classic cars, automobile fans can go to the Concours d'Elegance at Meadow Brook Hall, and to other festivals, such as those at the Henry Ford Museum and Greenfield Village. Both the museum and the village were created by Henry Ford and are located in Dearborn, a suburb of Detroit.

Henry Ford Museum has an amazing exhibit of American transportation, one of the finest anywhere. It includes classic and historic cars, trains, planes, and other forms of transport, plus a huge display of

American home life through the years. There are also many exhibits showing how America developed steam and electrical power for industrial and home use.

Behind the museum in Greenfield Village, visitors go back in time. The laboratory of Thomas Alva Edison, the homes of famous Americans such as Stephen Foster and Noah Webster, and a courthouse where Abraham Lincoln worked as a young attorney are all open for touring. The village also features a working windmill, a flour mill, and the Wright Brothers Bicycle Shop—all explained by guides in period costume. A highlight of the year is the Muzzleloaders Festival. In this event, black-powder shooters from all over the United States compete against each other with antique rifles.

Greenfield Village has special events for children of all ages. Village guides demonstrate the kinds of toys used by children of earlier times. Visitors are encouraged to try their hand at rolling hoops, walking on stilts, and quieter games.

Detroiters of all ages enjoy the high-speed excitement of the Grand Prix Formula I race—the only one in the United States. In June competitors come from around the world to test their driving skills on Detroit's course, which winds through the downtown area. Detroiters line the streets and watch from private parties in tall buildings to catch a glimpse of the racers. For a minute or two, all is

Black-powder shooters compete at the Muzzleloaders Festival.

A high-speed power boat roars along the Detroit River during the Spirit of Detroit race.

quiet. Then the roar of the engines grows louder and louder as the racers speed through the streets. One car flashes by, then another and another.

Detroit also hosts another race in June, but this one takes place on the Detroit River. In the Spirit of Detroit-Budweiser Thunderboats race, sleek, high-speed power boats turn the river white with foam. When the race boats leave, Detroiters also enjoy riding on boats that aren't quite that fast.

During the summer, two Boblo Island boats carry passengers to Boblo

A historic steamer carries passengers to Boblo Island Amusement Park.

Island Amusement Park at the south end of the Detroit River. On the island, visitors can choose from more than 75 rides and other attractions. On one weekend each year, the two boats hold their own annual riverboat race to see which one is the fastest.

Another favorite place to have fun is Belle Isle, a large park at the north end of the river that can be reached by driving over a bridge. There, Detroiters can fish, picnic, and see the oldest freshwater aquarium in the United States. They can also explore exhibits at the Dossin Great Lakes Museum, wild animals at the Belle Isle Zoo, and beautiful plants at the Whitcomb Conservatory.

Detroit has more than 6,000 acres (2,400 hectares) of parks, play-grounds, and playing fields, as well as beaches such as Metro Beach on Lake Saint Clair. River Rouge Park, the city's largest, has swimming pools, tennis courts, and a golf course. At Chene Park on the riverfront, Detroiters listen to concerts by the Detroit Symphony and other groups all summer long.

On Labor Day weekend, the city welcomes musicians from around the world for the Montreux Jazz Festival. There are free concerts at Hart Plaza and late-night jam sessions. At this popular event, the world's best jazz musicians perform and help other musicians learn through workshops.

For those who prefer a different kind of fun, the University Cultural Center is the place to be. Clustered

The roller coaster is one of the exciting rides on Boblo Island.

Detroiters relax on the grass during a concert at Chene Park.

around Wayne State University are 17 institutions that offer art, history, ethnic traditions, and scientific exploration. One of them is the Detroit Institute of Arts, which has one of the nation's top art collections. The Detroit Science Center encourages vis- itors to get involved with the exhibits and test out scientific principles for themselves.

Although it is not part of the Cultural Center, Cranbrook Academy's science museum offers much the same experience. Here, children search for

The Children's Museum is one of the institutions of the University Cultural Center.

fossils, test how light bends, learn about scientific puzzles, and watch the movement of the earth create designs in sand.

Another part of the University Cultural Center is the Children's Museum, which offers hands-on exhibits of cultural items from Michigan and the nation to help visitors understand history. The museum also offers workshops after school.

Pewabic Pottery is a popular place for those who enjoy ceramic arts. Here, students produce beautiful tiles

Examples of ceramic arts are on display at Pewabic Pottery.

and other pottery items. The Gallery exhibits some of the best in traditional and experimental pottery.

Detroiters can also visit the city's famous zoo, which houses more than 1,200 animals in natural settings similar to their homes in the wild. Visitors especially like the penguinarium and the new chimpanzee house.

For many Detroiters, fun and excitement mean sports. Detroit boasts a number of teams that have been champions at one time or another. Tiger Stadium is home to the Detroit Tigers,

Baseball fans cheer for the Detroit Tigers at Tiger Stadium.

World Series winners in 1984. The Detroit Lions belong to the National Football League and play at Pontiac Silverdome, a 45-minute drive from downtown. The Silverdome is the nation's largest air-supported dome stadium and can seat 80,000 people. It is also home to the Detroit Pistons basketball team.

Detroiters also go to Joe Louis Arena to watch the Red Wings play hockey. Concerts, shows, and sporting events are held in this arena and Cobo Hall, which are city landmarks. Joe Louis was a famous boxer in the 1930s, and he has a special place in the hearts of Detroiters.

Detroit's many sports fans reflect the competitive nature of this city's residents. While Detroit has had its share of problems, it also has the ability to "rise from its ashes," as the city seal says. As far as Detroiters are concerned, they live in the best city there is—and they intend to see that it keeps getting better.

A tugboat sends streams of water into the air during the International Freedom Festival.

Places to Visit in Detroit

Belle Isle
East Jefferson Avenue at East Grand Boulevard
(313) 267-7115
Includes Belle Isle Aquarium (267-7159)

Boblo Island Amusement Park
Veterans Memorial Building
151 West Jefferson Suite 714
(313) 843-8800
Boats leave from docks near Cobo Hall

Chene Park
In Rivertown at the foot of Chene Street
(313) 399-7001

Children's Museum
67 East Kirby
(313) 494-1210

Cranbrook Institute of Science/Academy of
Art Museum
500 Lone Pine Road
Bloomfield Hills, Michigan
(313) 645-3210/3323

Detroit Free Press Newspaper Tours
321 West Lafayette Building
(313) 222-8655

Detroit Historical Museum
5401 Woodward Avenue
(313) 833-1805

Detroit Institute of Arts
5200 Woodward Avenue
(313) 833-7900

Detroit Mounted Police Tours
100 East Bethune
(313) 876-0060

Detroit Red Wings
Joe Louis Arena
600 Civic Center Drive
(313) 567-6000

Detroit Science Center
5020 John Road
(313) 577-8400

Detroit Symphony
Ford Auditorium
(313) 567-1400

Detroit Tigers
Tiger Stadium
Trumbull at Michigan Avenue
(313) 962-4000

Detroit Zoological Park
Ten Mile Road at Woodward Avenue
Royal Oak, Michigan
(313) 398-0903

Dossin Great Lakes Museum
100 Strand, Belle Isle
(313) 267-6440

Eastern Market
2934 Russell
(313) 833-1560
Open-air market with flowers and produce

Fisher Theater
Fisher Building
West Grand Boulevard at Second Avenue
(313) 872-1000

Henry Ford Museum and Greenfield Village
20900 Oakwood Boulevard
Dearborn, Michigan
(313) 271-1620

Henry Ford Estate—Fair Lane
University of Michigan
Dearborn Campus
4901 Evergreen Road
Dearborn, Michigan
(313) 593-5590

Historic Fort Wayne
6325 West Jefferson Avenue
(313) 297-9360

International Institute
111 East Kirby
(313) 871-8600

Michigan Opera Theater
Detroit Music Hall
6519 Second Avenue
(313) 874-7850

Motown Museum
2648 West Grand Boulevard
(313) 875-2264

Museum of African-American History
301 Frederick
(313) 899-2500

Old Mariner's Church
170 East Jefferson Avenue
(313) 259-2206

Pewabic Pottery
10125 East Jefferson Avenue
(313) 822-0954

Renaissance Center
1 Jefferson Avenue
(313) 568-5626

Additional information can be obtained from these agencies:

Metropolitan Detroit Convention and Visitors Bureau
100 Renaissance Center Suite 1950
(313) 567-1170

Michigan Travel Bureau
Lansing, Michigan
1-800-543-2937

Detroit: A Historical Time Line

1701   Antoine de la Mothe Cadillac lands on what is now the Civic Center in downtown Detroit and opens a fur trading settlement

1760   The British gain control of Detroit during the French and Indian War

1796   The British give up Detroit to the new United States of America, and Detroit is named county seat of Wayne County

1805   Fire destroys the city's 200 structures, except stone warehouse

1812   The British briefly capture Detroit during the War of 1812, then Detroit becomes a permanent American possession and begins to grow dramatically

1815   Detroit incorporates as a city

1837   Michigan is admitted to the Union and Detroit becomes the capital; the city becomes a stop on the Underground Railroad

1860   Detroit supplies Union troops during the Civil War; major race riots break out in the city

1896   Henry Ford builds his first car

1903   Ford Motor Company is established

1920s   Two million foreign-born Detroit residents work in the auto industry

1935   The Detroit Tigers win the World Series

1937   Joe Louis, the "Brown Bomber," wins the world's heavyweight boxing championship

1940s	Detroit becomes the Arsenal of Democracy with massive war production
1951	Detroit celebrates its 250th birthday
1967	New Detroit is founded as the United States' first "urban coalition" to improve the city following the worst race riots ever
1974	Coleman Young takes office as Detroit's first black mayor
1977	Renaissance Center opens as a symbol of the city's rebirth
1982	First Grand Prix held
1984	Tigers win the World Series again
1987	The Detroit People Mover, an elevated railway, opens in downtown
1988	Detroit City Airport begins offering commercial passenger service; previously, it only served private aviation, with Detroit International Airport to the south handling commercial flights

Index